Decisions at the Water's Edge:

Sustaining Riparian Landscapes in the Midwest

Lynne M. Westphal and Michael E. Ostry

ACKNOWLEDGMENTS

The research findings described in this report stem from a sustained effort among Station scientists and collaborators since the inception of the Riparian Landscapes Integrated Research and Development Program in 1998. Those playing a critical part in shaping the program included Tom Crow, Linda Donoghue, Sue Barro, Dave Bengston, Dan Dey, John Dwyer, Paul Gobster, Jud Isebrands, Pamela Jakes, Randy Kolka, Brian Palik, Don Riemenschneider, Thomas Schmidt, Herb Schroeder, Steve Shifley, Dave Shriner, Stephanie Snyder, Susan Stewart, Frank Thompson, Elon S. (Sandy) Verry, and Pat Zollner.

Researchers contributing to the individual projects highlighted on these pages are cited in the text, with contact information provided in appendix 1. We are grateful for their participation in the Riparian Landscapes Program and for the opportunity to learn from them in our service as program co-leaders.

> *Where does the word "Riparian" come from? It's from Latin— "riparius"—which means of, on, or pertaining to the bank of a river, pond, or small lake.*

North Central Research Station
U.S. Department of Agriculture - Forest Service
1992 Folwell Avenue
Saint Paul, Minnesota 55108
2006
www.ncrs.fs.fed.us

Decisions at the Water's Edge: Sustaining Riparian Landscapes in the Midwest

A Progress Report

North Central Research Station
Sustaining Riparian Landscapes Integrated Research and Development Program

Lynne M. Westphal and Michael E. Ostry
Science Co-Leaders

Riparian areas in the Midwest Region include: land around smaller lakes (top), ponds (middle), and smaller rivers and creeks (bottom).

EXECUTIVE SUMMARY

Few regions in the country have a greater abundance of lakes, rivers, streams, wetlands, and their associated forested riparian areas than the seven States of the Midwest region. In developing an integrated approach to issues in the region's riparian areas, we are seeking answers to the following important questions for policymakers, planners, and managers:

1. How much riparian area do we have?
2. Who's using riparian areas and what's happening to these areas?
3. How do we rehabilitate riparian areas?

We can now partially answer these questions.

How much riparian area do we have? Although determining how much riparian area we have seems like a simple task, it's not. The process is complicated by the crucial first step of defining what areas actually are riparian. The first-ever estimation of riparian lands in the Midwest region conducted by North Central Research Station (NCRS) scientists, indicates that 8 to 13 percent of the land base in the region is riparian, depending on the buffer width selected. Of this total, 72 percent supports forest or other relatively natural vegetation, 26 percent has been converted to agriculture, and less than 2 percent is in urban development. Alternate delineation methods can dramatically increase the amount of riparian lands—by two times more in some places. Almost half of the Midwest region's riparian areas are associated with wetlands.

Who's using riparian areas and what's happening to these areas? People and wildlife depend on riparian areas. Many riparian areas are special places for experiences that significantly enhance mental well-being. Many urban rivers provide new recreation opportunities for city dwellers who may have little access to rural riparian areas. However, the intensity of recreation and development in riparian areas may threaten their long-term ecological health.

We are developing a variety of tools for managers to protect and restore the health of riparian areas. One tool involves constructing riparian profiles to help managers identify future development hotspots and to show how forest buffers can mitigate competing land uses, provide habitat, and protect riparian areas. Computer models and new silvicultural techniques are other tools that can enhance timber production, improve regeneration, and protect critical habitat.

How do we rehabilitate riparian areas? Ecological classification maps we have developed will help identify which restoration tools or approaches can be used on various sites. Our research on industrial brownfields is showing us what it takes to restore the ecological health of these areas. Guidelines we have developed for accurately determining streambank elevation are assisting in riparian and stream restoration, enhancement, and stabilization efforts. We have developed easy-to-use guides to design and install culverts of the right size in the right location. Using these guidelines not only ensures culverts meet road crossing requirements but also increases the likelihood that streams will provide healthy habitat.

We at the North Central Research Station are continuing to address the questions outlined above as well as emerging questions that are important to the protection and use of riparian areas, the unique areas of transition between land and water.

Midwest riparian areas include both urban and rural lakes (above), streams, and wetlands along with ecologically friendly industrial sites (right and bottom).

CONTENTS

Decisions at the Water's Edge: Sustaining Riparian Landscapes in the Midwest

A Progress Report

Introduction

The Sustaining Riparian Landscapes Integrated Research and Development Program is one of three integrated research programs developed by the North Central Research Station in 2000. These programs were described in the Station's strategic plan, *The Nature of Tomorrow*, that outlined the research needed to guide decisionmakers in enhancing and sustaining our region's natural resources.

Riparian areas are where the land and surface water meet and influence each other. Few regions in the country have a greater abundance of lakes, rivers, streams, wetlands, and their associated riparian areas than the seven States of the Midwest region. The forests riparian areas in the West are important because they are rare; in our region, they are important because they are common. Common they may be, but that does not mean that these riparian areas are understood, or that they do not have unique characteristics. Three striking features of Midwest riparian areas are the intermix of riparian areas with working forests, the amount of home development in riparian areas, and the impact of rust-belt industries on urban riparian areas.

Riparian areas are vital to healthy ecosystems. Vegetation in these areas provides shade that cools the water, critical for some fish species. Coarse woody debris at the land/water intersection provides nutrients and shelter for wildlife and other organisms critical to ecosystem functioning. Plants, trees, and soils filter ground and surface water, playing a critical role in maintaining water quality. Riparian areas soak up and store excess rain and snowmelt, reducing flooding downstream. Such interactions take place not just at the water's edge, but also much further into the uplands, depending on local terrain and other conditions (fig. 1).

Riparian areas are also important to people as places to live, work, and play. Water is a primary draw for homebuilding, whether it is a first or second home. Hiking, biking, boating, fishing, wildlife observation, and other free-time activities have long been of interest, but in some riparian areas, particularly urban ones, these activities are rising again in popularity. The intensity of interest and use makes

Lynne M. Westphal is a Research Social Scientist and Project Leader, with the North Central Research Station, Evanston, IL, and **Michael E. Ostry** is a Research Plant Pathologist, with the North Central Research Station, St. Paul, MN.

ALL LIFE DEPENDS ON WATER — — AND CLEAN, ABUNDANT WATER DEPENDS, IN PART, ON HEALTHY RIPARIAN AREAS.

◆ Riparian areas are transition areas of land and water that link terrestrial and aquatic ecosystems.

◆ Riparian areas are critical for maintaining water quality.

◆ Riparian areas are diverse, supporting unique vegetation and providing critical habitat for many species of fish, mammals, birds, reptiles, amphibians, insects, and microorganisms.

◆ Riparian areas are in high demand for recreation, timber production, and home sites.

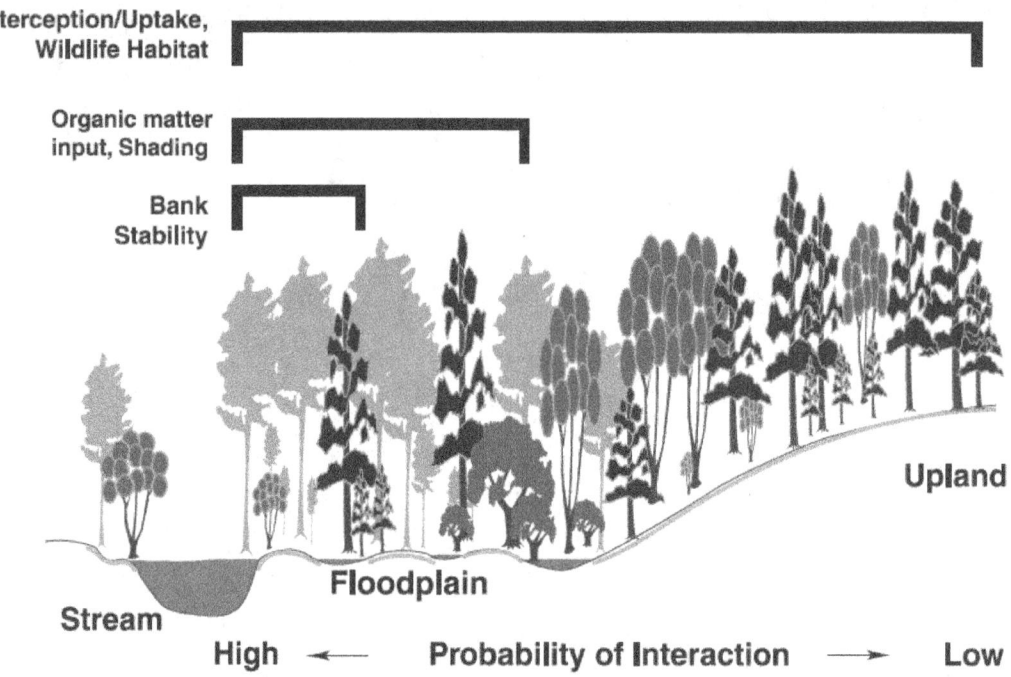

Figure 1.—*Stylized representation of a riparian area showing the lateral extent of various ecological interactions between land and water (Palik* et al. *2004).*

managing riparian areas difficult: we need to find ways to meet peoples expectations and preserve these important aspects of quality of life while also protecting the health and vitality of the lands themselves.

To determine how diverse land use in the Midwestern region affects riparian landscapes, we bring information from the physical, biological, and social sciences together to work across multiple scales ranging from single organisms to the landscape level. The program mission is *"Fostering multidisciplinary research to understand, predict, and monitor the effects of land use on the diverse benefits people gain from riparian areas."*

Our program is focused on the following questions:

(1) How much riparian area do we have?
(2) Who's using riparian areas and what's happening to these areas?
(3) How do we rehabilitate riparian areas?

Research on these issues is providing valuable information that policymakers and managers can use to make wise decisions at the water's edge. In this report we highlight some of our progress on what we have learned about riparian areas and we outline our future research directions.

GETTING AN ACCURATE COUNT: HOW MUCH RIPARIAN AREA DO WE HAVE?

To protect the many benefits provided by riparian areas, society has developed a variety of policies and guidelines to ensure that human activity does not harm riparian areas. Are we applying these policies to the right places? Keys to answering this question include a good definition and good measure of riparian areas. Because the accuracy of information used in making policy and management decisions about riparian areas can have significant ecological and economic implications, we need better tools for accurately delineating what is—and is not—riparian.

Estimating the Amount of Riparian Area

Station scientists and their collaborators have made the first-ever assessment of the extent of riparian areas in the Midwest. They used a variety of delineation methods and characterized the riparian areas as being residential, industrial, agricultural, or still natural. They used various regional and subregional data sources as they compared riparian extent and condition using 30- or 60-m-wide buffers.

They estimate that 8.9 to 13.2 million ha (30- and 60-m buffers, respectively) or 8 to 13 percent of the total land base in the region is riparian (fig. 2). Minnesota, Wisconsin, and Michigan account for nearly 77 percent of this total; 17 to 23 percent of the land in these three States is riparian (fig. 3). Native forest or other vegetation is supported on approximately 72 percent of the riparian lands in the region while 26 percent has been converted to agriculture and less than 2 percent to urban development.

Patterns of land use in riparian areas vary within the region, contrasting sharply between the Farm Belt States of Iowa, Illinois, Indiana, and Missouri and the Lake States of Minnesota, Wisconsin, and Michigan. Within the Lake States, 73 to 81 percent are natural/seminatural riparian areas compared to 38 to 55 percent in the Farm Belt States (fig. 4).

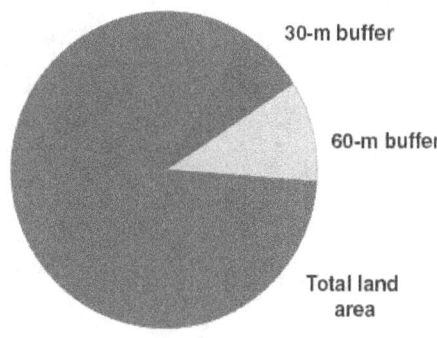

30-m buffer

60-m buffer

Total land area

Figure 2.—*Cumulative riparian area in the Midwest Region using 30-m buffers and the additional land included by extending buffers to 60-m (Palik et al. 2004).*

HOW MUCH RIPARIAN AREA DO WE HAVE?

◆ Depending on buffer width, 8 to 13 percent of the land base in the Midwest is riparian.

◆ Of the land classified as riparian in the Midwest, 72 percent supports native forest or other vegetation, 26 percent has been converted to agriculture, and less than 2 percent is in urban development.

◆ Alternate delineation methods can dramatically increase the amount of riparian lands—by more than two times in some places.

◆ Almost half of the riparian areas in the region are associated with wetlands rather than with streams, lakes, or rivers.

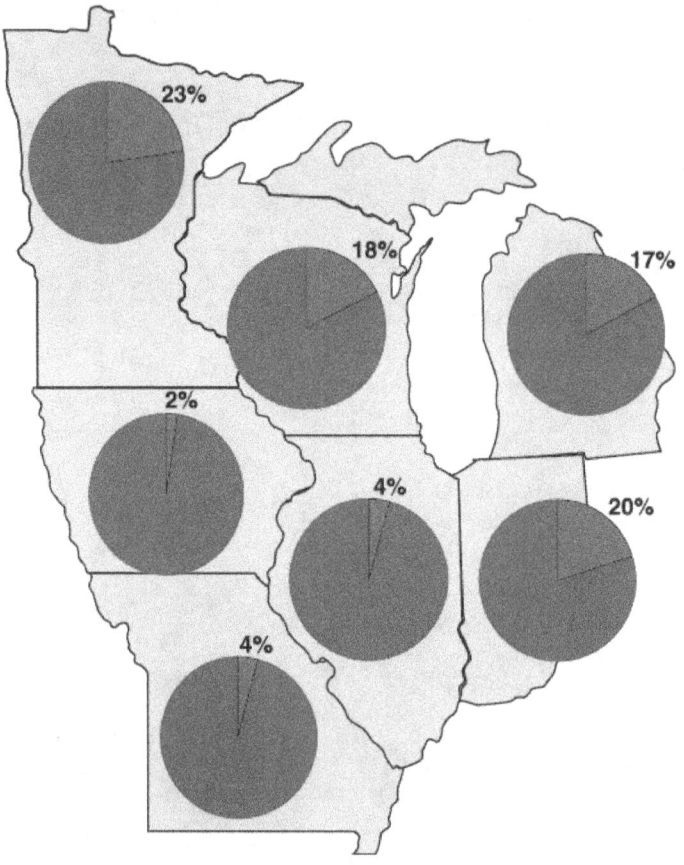

The assessment shows that with 30-m buffers, 36 percent of riparian areas are in stream and river corridors, 16 percent are associated with lakes, and 56 percent are associated with wetlands. This means that wetlands make up the largest proportion of riparian areas, but our understanding of the ecological functions and impacts of land use in these areas is incomplete and management guidelines are not well developed.

To understand Midwest riparian areas, we must understand wetlands. Some wetlands, however, are here today, gone tomorrow—or at least here this season, gone the next, only to return again. Seasonal wetlands of less than 0.5 ha are abundant in many forests, but their ecological importance and responses to disturbance of the surrounding upland areas are poorly understood. Because these wetlands are small and may be dry for periods of time, they are often overlooked, not included in wetland assessments, and subject to potentially degrading impacts during upland management operations. Determining the location of seasonal wetlands is a key challenge for resource managers—especially given the forest management guidelines that dictate protecting them. By using land type associations and glacial landforms, Station scientists have been able to predict the occurrence of seasonal wetlands within a large forested landscape. Using this approach, managers will be able to anticipate the occurrence of these wetlands and take necessary precautions to avoid impacting them during management operations.

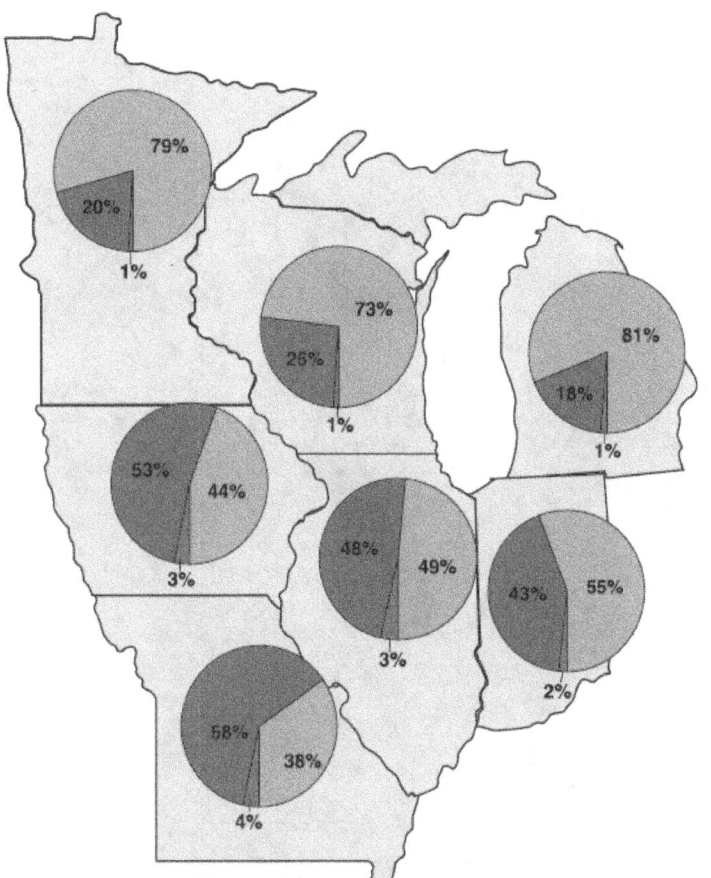

Figure 4.—*Riparian land use in the Midwest Region. Colors represent percentages of riparian lands in different land cover categories (red is agriculture, gold is natural land cover, blue is urban/developed) (Palik* et al. *2004).*

A fixed-width buffer approach for delineating riparian areas is expedient but does not capture the true variable nature of riparian areas on the ground. Therefore, Station scientists are exploring alternative means of defining riparian areas that rely less on expediency and more on accuracy. One approach looks at the topography of floodplains for clues, and another approach looks beyond the floodplain for other geomorphic clues to riparian delineation.

Delineating riparian areas based on the width of flood-prone areas creates very different riparian areas, depending on the shape of the valley. A narrow valley between steeper hills will have a narrower riparian zone compared

to a broad, flat stream valley with a wide floodplain (figs. 5 and 6). On the whole, this more functionally based delineation method leads to significantly increased estimates of riparian area in a watershed. For example, a pilot test of this method in several watersheds in Minnesota revealed that the variable-width approach increased riparian area estimates by 100 to 170 percent over estimates based on 60-m buffers.

But we have evidence that riparian areas can extend beyond even the floodplain. Station scientists investigated an old-growth northern hardwood watershed. They found that over half of the major shifts in ground flora communities in the stream valley and nearly all of

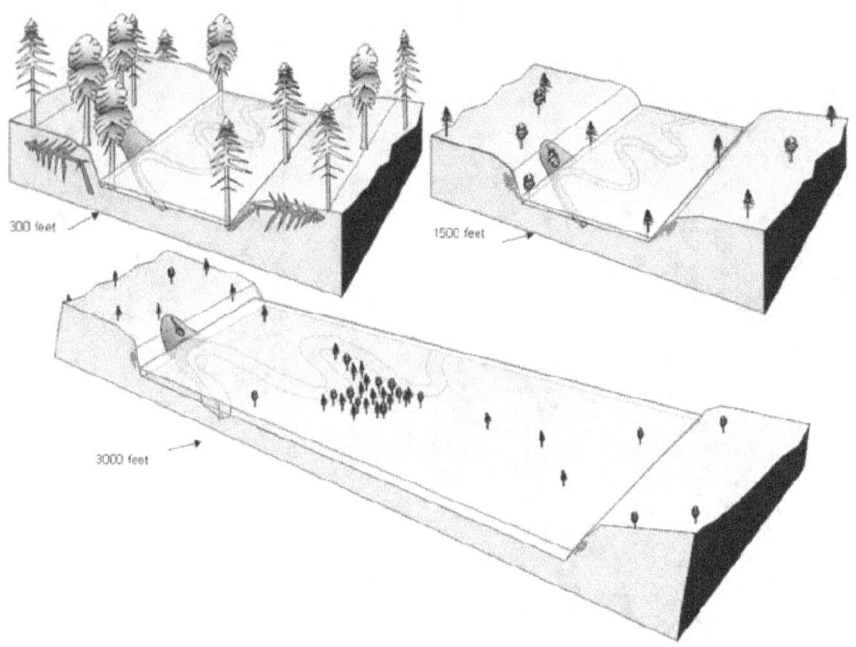

Figure 5.—*Example of the Riparian Ecotone definition (red boundary) in three alluvial valleys. (Photo credit: Sandy Verry)*

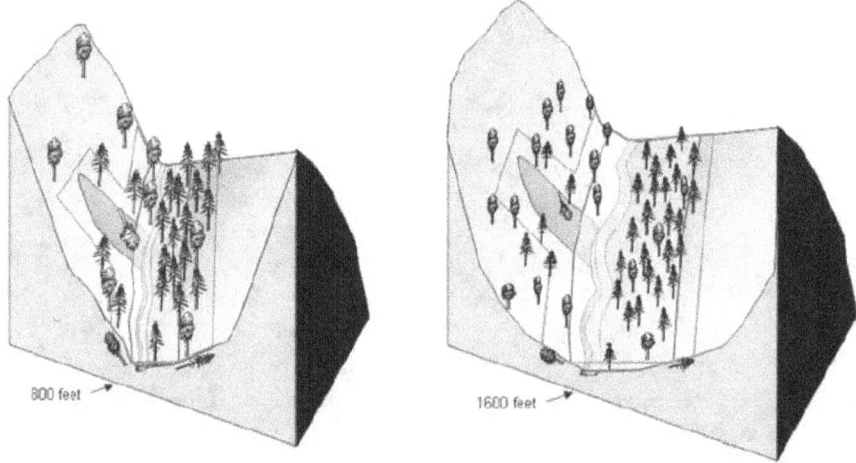

Figure 6.—*Example of the riparian ecotone definition (red boundary) in V-shaped valleys. (Photo credit: Sandy Verry)*

the shifts in the overstory composition occurred beyond the influence of flooding. This suggests that it might not be flooding as much as other processes such as glacial soil deposition that control vegetation communities across stream valleys. Therefore, expanding riparian management zones to include these unique areas is an important policy and management step.

Our next steps in developing more precise methods to delineate riparian areas will build on these recent advancements: clues from geology and topography and elsewhere that can help us develop functional methods, rather than expedient, fixed-width methods, for riparian area delineation. The better we get at delineation, the more finely tuned—and effective—our policies can become.

To understand Midwest riparian areas, we must understand wetlands.

WHO'S USING RIPARAIAN AREAS AND WHAT'S HAPPENING TO THESE AREAS?

Who is using riparian areas? Industry; agriculture; timber producers; home developers; recreationists; birds, fish, and other wildlife. The intensity of riparian use can threaten the ecological integrity of this resource. Industry, agriculture, home development, and recreation threaten the habitat that birds, fish, and other animals, insects, and plants need to survive. Dams, levees, and channelization of streams and rivers reduce or eliminate seasonal flooding essential in maintaining habitat that is crucial for wildlife. Increasing environmental concern and the laws and regulations created to address these concerns impact riparian areas and their use. One of these impacts is increased restrictions on timber harvesting in riparian areas.

What can make riparian areas particularly difficult to plan for and manage is that this wide range of interests is often focused on a single stretch of river or lake shore. Home development, recreation use, industrial use, and important wildlife habitat can all overlap. Even within each interest area there can be diverse views that do not always fit easily together. Birding and fishing may or may not be compatible in the same riparian spot. New home developments might limit traditional access to a lake. These and other overlapping interests make life interesting, to say the least.

The good news is that research findings are helping to guide land use and land management decisions, and as a result environmental laws and changes in policy are improving these conditions. For example, Station scientists have demonstrated that it is possible to harvest timber in riparian zones without degrading ecological conditions. Cut-to-length harvest methods result in greater aspen regeneration than other methods while minimizing soil and residual tree disturbance. These and other results have been incorporated into riparian zone guidelines that are being used by many State and Federal agencies.

Major environmental laws have led to cleaner rivers and streams, leading in turn to renewed use of these waterways for recreation. Industries can no longer discharge untreated water into wetlands, rivers, and streams. Green development ideas are catching on: more often stormwater is handled in vegetated swales rather than sewers, roofs are planted with sedum instead of covered in tar. These changes create meaningful improvements in both riparian health and broader ecological health.

WHO'S USING RIPARIAN AREAS AND WHAT'S HAPPENING TO THESE AREAS?

◆ Many riparian areas are special places for experiences that significantly enhance mental well-being.

◆ Riparian profiles help managers identify future development hotspots.

◆ Forest buffers can mitigate competing land uses, provide wildlife habitat, and protect riparian areas.

◆ Computer models and silvicultural techniques can enhance timber production, improve regeneration, and protect critical habitat. These models show that the rate of harvest is the key factor.

◆ It is possible to harvest in riparian zones without causing ecological damage, if done carefully. For example, cut-to-length harvest methods result in greater aspen regeneration than other methods while also minimizing soil and residual tree disturbance.

Another important question about riparian areas is this: what is happening to riparian health because of human use? In our research we have investigated the important experiences that riparian areas offer people and the means of protecting riparian areas for these experiences as well as for wildlife and habitat. This is a part of balancing the desire for use and the need for ecological health. We also have developed tools to help understand and predict the pressures on riparian areas, including computer modeling to understand forest operation impacts as well as to predict the likely locations for new housing developments.

Riparian Areas are Often Special Places

Many riparian areas are special places for recreation, providing unique benefits to residents and visitors. For example, research indicates that wooded trails near water provide better opportunities than other forested settings for reflection, intimate communication, privacy, and other experiences that are critical for psychological well-being. This can be particularly important in urban areas where once severely polluted rivers now offer opportunities for boating, fishing, and simple quiet moments watching the water flow by. In fact, both rural and urban riparian areas provide significant experiences, like serenity and the chance to "get connected to that which is important in...life."

We have developed and refined a set of tools and techniques that can provide useful information for managers about these unique places. We used focus groups and design workshops to reach consensus on a long needed makeover of a small section of Chicago's Lincoln Park, a place that was equally loved by birders, anglers, and landscape preservationists. At Midewin National Tallgrass Prairie, we asked local residents to take photographs of places in and around Midewin that were important to them and then used these photos to guide in-depth interviews with these residents. Using information revealed in the photos and interviews, we were able to help planners understand what was important to local residents as they developed their first prairie plan. It turned out that riparian places were very important to respondents, even in a relatively dry landscape.

Riparian Special Places: One of these quotes describes experiences in an urban riparian location, the other is from the Northwoods of Wisconsin. Can you tell which is which?

1. A river with a unique eddy creating a hole for brook trout. A mile walk through wet ... swamp .... Occasional sightings of raccoon, ... deer, heron and hawks. ... No easy spot to find, but is visited 4 times per trout season on the average. A spot discovered alone but since have found others know of it and have fished it. Only have encountered one other party there in 8 years. Complete privacy, solitude is relaxing.

2. Although I passed by frequently, I never noticed a big swamp through the trees and down the hill until a friend showed me an obscure path down to it. Now, throughout the year, I sit immobile on a fallen tree and watch deer, muskrats and beavers. ... I never encounter another soul there, yet friends tell me they have visited. The people who go there treat the site with awe and respect. ... It's a tiny, private undiscovered place where I can go all by myself to chill out and get reconnected to that which is important in my life.

1 is from the northwoods, 2 is from an urban area.

Riparian Buffers Provide Numerous Benefits

Buffers along rivers, lakes, and wetlands can provide many benefits and are therefore the focus of many policies. We have been exploring the ways in which buffers can both provide critical habitat and cushion different land uses (fig. 7). For example, buffers can help improve water quality, and hybrid poplars in buffers can filter agricultural runoff and provide a cash crop for farmers.

Populations of many songbirds have been dwindling for decades, and loss of habitat is a primary culprit in their decline. Riparian forests provide habitat for unique species and often have greater species richness and abundance of birds than upland forests; for this reason they are considered a conservation priority. In the Midwest, many riparian forests exist as corridors along rivers in landscapes dominated by agricultural land uses. The highly fragmented nature of these forests can provide hostile conditions for birds resulting in high nest predation and brood parasitism by brown-headed cowbirds. Field research by Station scientists determined how characteristics of riparian forest corridors, such as width and vegetation structure, affected songbird abundance and nest success. Extensive forested riparian corridors provided breeding habitat for more bird species than basic riparian corridors. The addition of planted grassland-shrub buffer strips

adjacent to the forest increased species richness and densities of grassland-shrub nesting species. There was also some evidence that planted grassland-shrub buffer strips reduced nest predation in riparian corridors, possibly because they "softened" the typically "hard" edge between cropland and forest that may be used as a travel lane by predators.

Buffers can also address one of the consequences of urban sprawl: increased contact between new residential developments and working farms. This close association too often

Extensive forested riparian corridors provide breeding habitat for more bird species than basic riparian corridors.

results in conflicts that both farmers and the new residents would prefer to avoid. To farmers, land is the foundation for the business of agriculture. But for urbanites who settle outside of central cities because they enjoy the open space and bucolic environment of the agricultural landscape, the normal operation of a modern farm—complete with dust, noise, and smells—is often a source of tension. One possible, albeit partial, solution is to alter the connection between active farms and housing by planting landscape buffers. But will residents who sought out an agricultural neighbor object to a change in the landscape that might block their view of farms? Or to the sunrise or sunset? And what about farmers? Will farmers

No Buffer

Basic Buffer

Extensive Buffer

Figure 7.—A typical photo simulation, in this case showing a riparian forest buffer from the ground (top images) and from the air (bottom images), at three levels: no buffer, basic, and extensive.

object to the introduction of buffers that might shade their fields, harbor weeds, and attract animals? We investigated and found that both farmers and residents approve of buffers. Overall, wide buffers received the highest approval ratings, and residents' approval ratings of them were significantly higher than those of farmers. These findings have implications for public policy. They show that landscape buffers—features that can help reduce land use conflicts at the rural-urban fringe—are considered not only acceptable, but also desirable by local stakeholders (fig. 8). These findings also suggest that communities that are growing at the rural-urban fringe could use landscape buffers as social buffers.

Landscape buffers—features that can help reduce land use conflicts at the rural-urban fringe—are considered not only acceptable, but also desirable by local stakeholders

The amount of riparian buffer might be easier to increase than one might think. In fact, due in part to agricultural policy, we now have more agricultural land riparian buffers in some places than we did decades ago. What is needed is additional input to policies that encourage buffers so that they provide as many benefits as possible—improved water quality, habitat, and peace between neighbors.

Computer Models Can Assist Decisionmakers

Computer modeling can help us understand impacts of land use choices, from timber harvest to development plans. For example, Station scientists have developed computer-based spatial-analytical tools that allow resource managers to evaluate the potential ecological effects of proposed forest management plans and weigh different options. In one study, researchers investigated forest operations and salamanders. Salamanders are a good indicator species because they are an important link in the food chain in forest ecosystems and are sensitive to changes in moisture caused by timber harvesting operations. Our computer model related forest conditions and topography to abundance of salamanders, which in turn pointed to habitat quality. It turned out that the key factor in salamander abundance was the rate of harvest, not the shape or location of the harvest areas.

Computer tools can be useful in assessing the impacts of development, too. With our support, researchers at the University of Michigan developed a process to simulate landscapes and integrate land use/land cover data. The researchers developed landscape-level indicators that can be used for evaluating the potential impact of development on aquatic ecosystems.

Figure 8.—*Approval ratings for three levels of buffer by three groups of stakeholders. Extensive buffers received the highest approval ratings, but residents' approval ratings of them were significantly higher than those of farmers.*

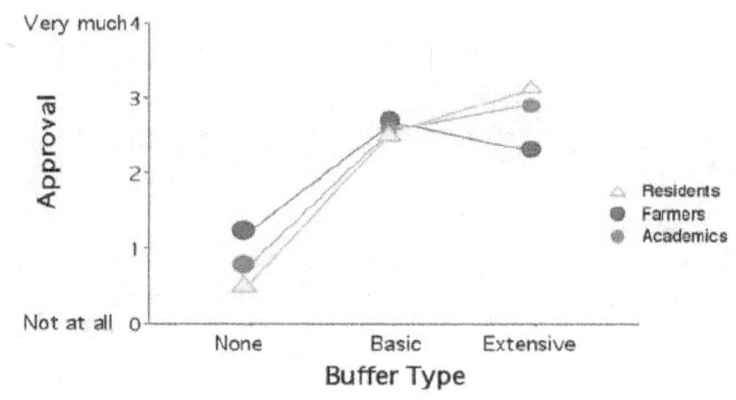

Lake Management Profiles Can Predict Future Development Impacts

All too often, planners and managers are left responding to the impacts of development after it has occurred. Figure 9 shows the lakeshore development in Three Lakes, Wisconsin, between 1938 and 1998. Imagine if, in 1938, Three Lakes Township planners could have foreseen the development that was coming. Being able to plan would have been an immense help in protecting important habitats. With this in mind, Station scientists and others developed a way to identify lake development hotspots. They created lake riparian development profiles that allow planners to compare all lakes in a region and identify lakes with fewer barriers to development.

The profiles (fig. 10) are built from readily available, mappable information describing physical and social characteristics important to development. These include:
  (1) dwelling density,
  (2) percent riparian area developed,
  (3) potential development limitations (a characteristic that combines information on the soils' suitability for construction and the distance to an existing road),
  (4) percent private ownership,
  (5) aesthetic appeal (a characteristic that combines information on beach soils and vegetation), and
  (6) distance to a retail center.

For example, imagine two lakes, Blue Lake and Clear Lake. They are similar in many respects except that Blue Lake's undeveloped riparian area has soils that will not support the construction of roads or septic systems while Clear Lake's undeveloped riparian area has soils that will support construction. New development will most likely occur around Clear Lake before it occurs around Blue Lake. Land use planners looking to manage or direct development would want to concentrate first on the development potential of Clear Lake, then consider Blue Lake.

Currently, the test-run profiles developed for Itasca County, Minnesota, are being used by the Itasca County Soil and Water Conservation Service in developing new regulations on residential growth in riparian areas, and by the Chippewa National Forest in revising the forest management plan.

As we said earlier—everyone is using riparian areas, in ways they recognize (streamside walks) and ways they may not (high quality drinking water). The impacts on riparian lands need to be fully understood and, where necessary, mitigated. Tools like lake development profiles, computer models, and riparian buffers can help balance the many demands made on riparian areas.

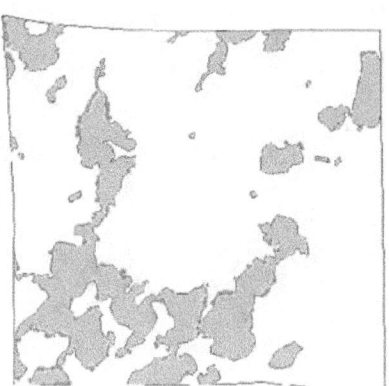 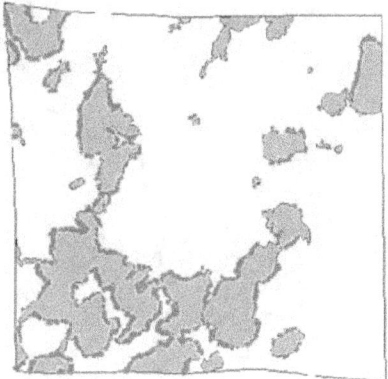

Figure 9.—*Housing locations and housing density changes in riparian areas in Three Lakes Township, Oneida County, Wisconsin, 1938 (left) and 1998 (right). Each red dot indicates one house. (Graphic created by Charlotte Gonzolez-Abraham, University of Wisconsin-Madison.)*

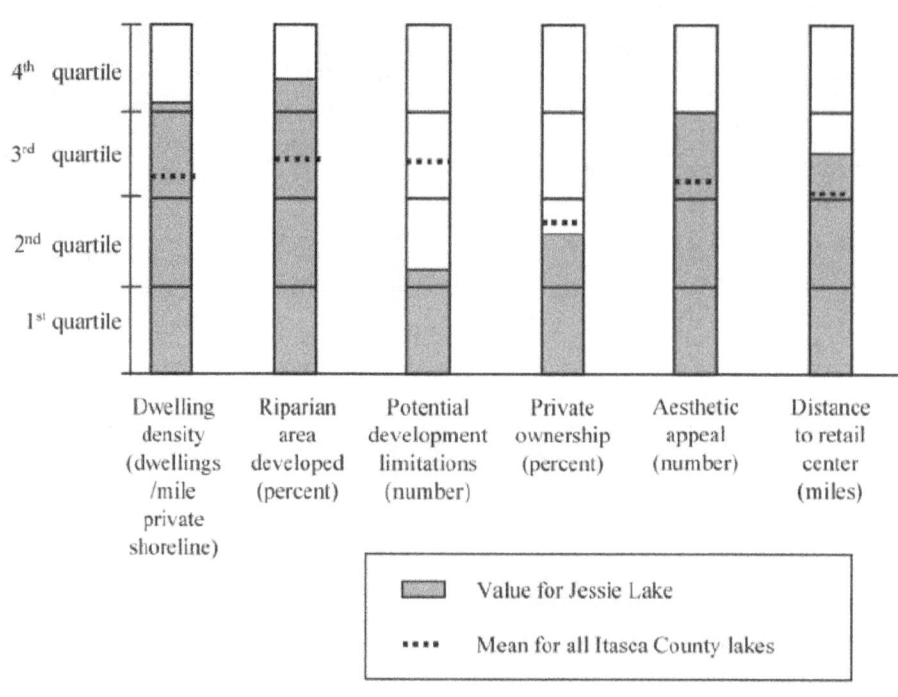

4th quartile

3rd quartile

2nd quartile

1st quartile

Dwelling
density
(dwellings
/mile
private
shoreline)

Riparian
area
developed
(percent)

Potential
development
limitations
(number)

Private
ownership
(percent)

Aesthetic
appeal
(number)

Distance
to retail
center
(miles)

Value for Jessie Lake

Mean for all Itasca County lakes

*A common sight around the Midwest region are second home
developments in and around riparian areas.*

This Old Ditch: How Do We Rehabilitate Riparian Areas?

Many of our riparian areas need help. We are living with the consequences of past human actions that have resulted in degraded habitat, increased erosion, and more frequent and severe flooding. Restoration and rehabilitation, however, are anything but easy. What works in one place may not work in another. There may be a suite of seemingly incompatible needs and interests to be accommodated in a single restoration project. Ecological rehabilitation and restoration is a new science and art, about which we have much to learn. Our research over the past few years has added to the knowledge and understanding of restoration and ecological rehabilitation.

Often the word "restoration" implies a return to pre-European settlement conditions. A growing number of scientists question whether this is possible. For instance, with the climate changes of the past century, even if we were able to remove every building and road and bring back every plant and animal, the current climate may no longer support those earlier assemblages in exactly the same way. In heavily developed areas, returning to pre-settlement conditions is often an unattainable goal for pragmatic reasons: these ecological systems are so fragmented, so heavily impacted, and in other ways so severely altered from those found by the first Europeans arriving in the Midwest that a return to earlier days is impractical, if not impossible. But some ecological rehabilitation is possible. We can almost always improve existing conditions and foster healthy, functioning, thriving ecosystems, whether we are in the midst of a major metropolitan area or in a remote forest. It is with this spirit that the Sustaining Riparian Landscapes Integrated Program approaches rehabilitation of Midwest riparian areas—we believe that we can make a positive difference.

Where in the (Ecological) World am I?

What makes a restoration technique work really well in one place but fail at another site nearby? Two places near each other as the crow flies can differ greatly in ecological terms, and these differences can indicate the need for different restoration tools. Therefore, one key piece of information in planning ecological rehabilitation is understanding a site's place in the ecological world. Ecological hierarchical assessments show which areas are similar at different scales. NCRS scientists have contributed to these systems by developing the aquatic zoogeographic ecological classification system (fig. 11). These maps show related aquatic habitats from broad zones to individual streams. Assessments are based on the distribution of native fish species, following watershed and subwatershed boundaries. These maps can show which kind of sub-ecosystem a riparian site is in, which, in turn, can help determine whether a restoration tool used on a project in one place might be applicable to a project in another place—or whether it might fail.

REHABILITATING RIPARIAN LANDSCAPES

◆ Our ecological classification maps can help determine a site's ecological "type" and help predict if restoration tools or approaches used elsewhere might also work there.

◆ Riparian and stream restoration, enhancement, and stabilization depend on accurately determining stream bankfull elevation, but this is harder than it seems. Our guidelines show how to do it right.

◆ We have developed easy-to-use guides to design and install culverts to meet road crossing requirements *and* support healthy habitat.

◆ Understanding social assets provides key ways to connect agencies and nongovernmental organizations with local residents.

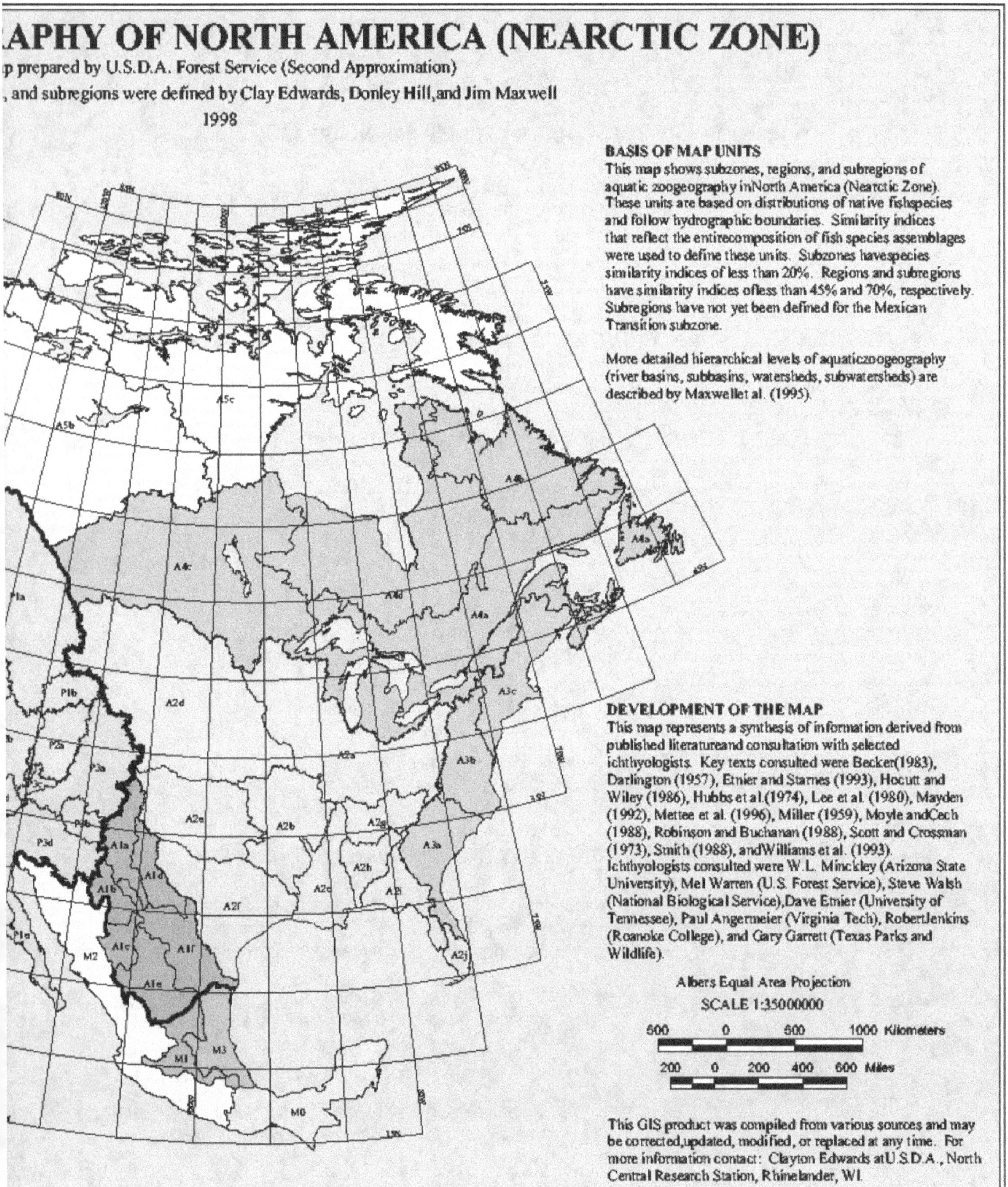
APHY OF NORTH AMERICA (NEARCTIC ZONE)
p prepared by U.S.D.A. Forest Service (Second Approximation)
, and subregions were defined by Clay Edwards, Donley Hill,and Jim Maxwell
1998
BASIS OF MAP UNITS
This map shows subzones, regions, and subregions of aquatic zoogeography inNorth America (Nearctic Zone). These units are based on distributions of native fishspecies and follow hydrographic boundaries. Similarity indices that reflect the entirecomposition of fish species assemblages were used to define these units. Subzones havespecies similarity indices of less than 20%. Regions and subregions have similarity indices ofless than 45% and 70%, respectively. Subregions have not yet been defined for the Mexican Transition subzone.
More detailed hierarchical levels of aquaticzoogeography (river basins, subbasins, watersheds, subwatersheds) are described by Maxwellet al. (1995).
A5c
A5b
A4b
A4c
A4d
A4a
A3c
A3b
A3a
A2d
A2a
A2e
A2b
A2g
A2h
A2c
A2i
A2f
A2j
P1a
P1b
P2a
P3a
P3d
P1e
A1a
A1b
A1d
A1c
A1f
A1e
M1
M2
M3
M0
DEVELOPMENT OF THE MAP
This map represents a synthesis of information derived from published literatureand consultation with selected ichthyologists. Key texts consulted were Becker(1983), Darlington (1957), Etnier and Starnes (1993), Hocutt and Wiley (1986), Hubbs et al.(1974), Lee et al. (1980), Mayden (1992), Mettee et al. (1996), Miller (1959), Moyle andCech (1988), Robinson and Buchanan (1988), Scott and Crossman (1973), Smith (1988), andWilliams et al. (1993). Ichthyologists consulted were W.L. Minckley (Arizona State University), Mel Warren (U.S. Forest Service), Steve Walsh (National Biological Service),Dave Etnier (University of Tennessee), Paul Angermeier (Virginia Tech), RobertJenkins (Roanoke College), and Gary Garrett (Texas Parks and Wildlife).
Albers Equal Area Projection
SCALE 1:35000000
500 0 500 1000 Kilometers
200 0 200 400 600 Miles
This GIS product was compiled from various sources and may be corrected,updated, modified, or replaced at any time. For more information contact: Clayton Edwards atU.S.D.A., North Central Research Station, Rhinelander, WI.

Figure 11.—Aquatic zoogeography of North America (nearctic zone)

From Landscape Level to Microsite: The Importance of Culvert Placement for Riparian Health

The seemingly simple act of placing a culvert can have surprising impacts on stream and riparian health. Placed improperly, culverts wreak havoc on the riparian landscape by increasing erosion, degrading habitat, and limiting fish spawning. Given the vast number of culverts, even minor damage by individual culverts have a dramatic, cumulative impact across the landscape. Therefore, to help restore and protect riparian areas, NCRS scientists have developed culvert placement guidelines that non-engineers can use for smaller crossings and professionals can use when placing larger culverts. These guidelines have been field-tested on 20 new culverts; 2 years of followup measurements show success. Culverts placed according to our guides keep soil in place, allow fish to reach spawning grounds, and will support roads for at least 50 years, thereby helping to transform an old ditch into a healthy stream or river (fig. 12a and b).

Figure 12a and b.—*Installation of an off-set culvert pair. The lower culvert is set into the stream bottom (about 1/6th of its diameter); the upper culvert is a foot higher. This allows low flows to occur in a narrow (and deeper) path where fish can pass more easily. The two culverts together should equal the bankfull channel width so that fish can pass during bankfull flows at velocities near 3 feet per second. A single culvert, equal to the bankfull channel width could have been used, but the low rise to the road surface suggested multiple culverts.*

Calumet: An Intricate Mix of Nature and Rust

The cornerstone of NCRS's recent riparian rehabilitation and restoration work has been our work as a part of the Calumet Initiative. The Calumet Initiative is a coalition of local residents, academia, government agencies, regional and local nongovernmental organizations, museums, and businesses. The Calumet region in northwest Indiana and northeast Illinois is a birthplace of both the study of ecology and industry (fig. 13). Henry Cowles, one of the founders of ecology, developed the theory of succession at Calumet's Indiana Dunes; U.S. Steel and other industries built their steel mills and other plants in Calumet in the late 1880s. Today, Calumet is a quintessential rustbelt area, yet many industries still thrive there (fig. 14). Paradoxically, numerous State-threatened and endangered species also flourish in Calumet—in remnant natural areas nestled among active and abandoned industrial plants. The Calumet region also draws recreationists hoping to see a rare bird, catch a big fish, or just enjoy the outdoors.

We are working with the many partners of the Calumet Initiative to help local and regional planners and managers decide how to move the Calumet region toward ecological **and** economic health. We provide information and technology in five key areas to help inform this dynamic, challenging process: roadmaps to recovery, ecotoxicity, eco-creativity, people-land connection, and an understanding of the interests of a heterogeneous population. To illustrate these areas, we highlight here information from just **four** of the many projects underway in Calumet.

Roadmaps to Recovery
Ecological recovery of a rustbelt landscape requires careful, strategic planning. We worked closely with Chicago's Department of Environment to create an Ecological Management Strategy (EMS) for the Calumet region of Chicago. The goal of the EMS is to develop a macroplan and strategy to improve the natural areas around Lake Calumet and then expand from there to the broader Calumet region.

In creating this strategy, stakeholders developed a framework for prioritizing ecological rehabilitation at individual riparian sites, identifying ecological attributes to *preserve*, *improve*, and *create* at each location. Site Attributes categorized as "preserve" and "improve" contain some aspect of the desired future condition such as viable marsh or rookery habitat. "Create" designates sub-sites so damaged that they provide opportunities to start almost from scratch, creating new habitat types. The "preserve, improve, create" analysis provides a decisionmaking structure for each site, facilitating choices among ecological rehabilitation tools; and it can be

Figure 13.—*The Calumet region of Illinois and Indiana.*

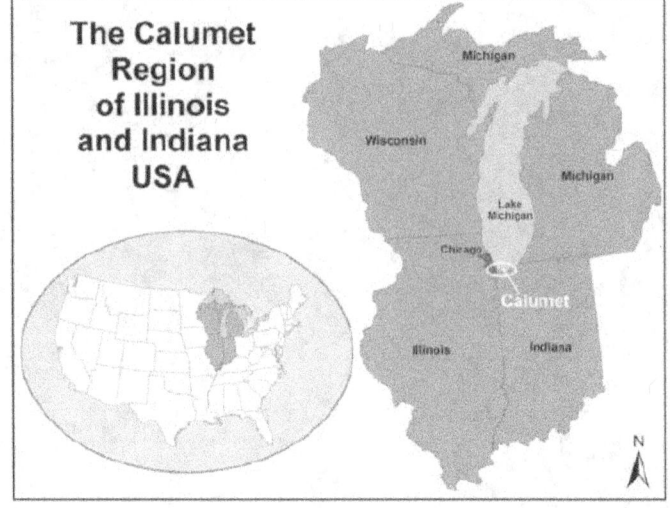

Figure 14.—*Calumet is home to industry, brownfields, and critical riparian habitat.*

transferred to other sites and ecological planning conundrums.

Eco-creativity leads to riparian reconstructive surgery

NCRS scientists have been leaders in bringing new health to human-altered streams and ditches, providing what amounts to reconstructive surgery for riparian areas.

The stream reconstruction process begins with analysis of the existing stream, particularly the bankfull levels (fig. 15). These can be difficult to determine but are critical to successful ecological rehabilitation. Station scientists and others have collaborated on guidelines for determining bankfull levels on streams in the Eastern United States. Other stream characteristics also are important: water chemistry, shape and sinuosity, sediment, and flow rate are all examined. These data are compared with those from a "natural" stream, and from these comparisons Station scientists develop detailed plans for creating the new, improved, stream.

One recent stream that received Station scientists' attention is Indian Creek in Calumet. This is an example of eco-creativity because Indian Creek is not a creek at all—it emerged as people filled in wetlands with slag and cinder, leaving a measly ditch instead of the acres of wetlands that nature created.

Figure 15.—*Stream restoration through reshaping: Indian Creek in Calumet.*

The Ford Motor Company has implemented the Station's plans for the segment of Indian Creek that runs on Ford's newly acquired land. Transformed from that measly ditch, Indian Creek's new design—pools and riffles, stream widths based on appropriate bankfull dimensions, and improved sinuosity—is creating aquatic and riparian habitat that brings new ecological health to the site. Local anglers will catch more fish, and kids will have better chances to find tadpoles and other aquatic creatures.

Eco-toxicity: Is phytoremediation a wonderful tool or potentially part of the problem?
In many ecological rehabilitation projects, site contamination must be addressed. This is true in both urban and rural locations. When natural areas are contaminated, or even when insects and other wildlife are exposed to less-than-natural contaminated sites, contaminants can move into the food chain resulting in problems for wildlife, plant species, and humans (e.g., mercury buildup in fish). The environmental impact, or potential impact, of toxicity from contaminated sites is sometimes referred to as eco-toxicity or "ecotox" for short.

Phytoremediation is one possible means of dealing with contamination, and thereby reducing the potential ecotox impacts of a polluted site. Phytoremediation harnesses the natural processes by which plants absorb, transport, and transform water and chemicals in their roots, stems, and leaves, to remove contaminants from soil and ground water. Matching plants to the contaminants they handle most effectively is the key element of phytoremediation design.

In Calumet, NCRS scientists conducted above-ground tank experiments testing the effectiveness of native willow, cottonwood, and switch grass in removing contaminants from Cluster Site soil and ground water (figs. 16 and 17). This research looked in part at whether species planted for phytoremediation will, in fact, clean up the target contaminants and improve site conditions. For example, some, but not all, cottonwoods can mitigate trichloroethylene, a common ground water pollutant.

But might phytoremediation move contaminants into the food chain? This is a serious concern in a place like Calumet, where there are important species and habitats to protect. To be an effective cleanup tool, phytoremediation cannot have unintended ecotox consequences like this. To begin to address this issue, the Calumet study includes a test of heavy metal accumulation in insects feeding on phytoremediation vegetation.

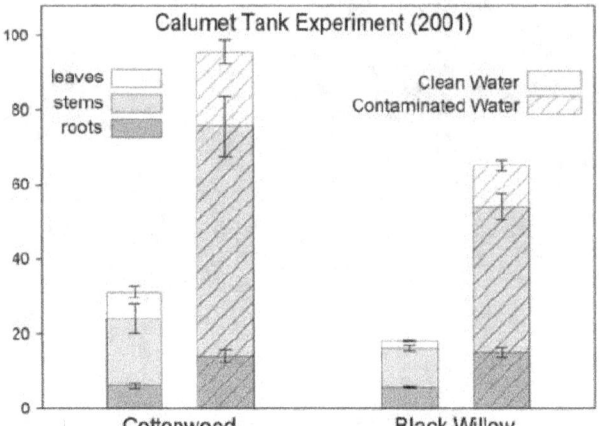

Figure 16.—*Final biomass of individual cottonwood and black willow trees growing in clean and contaminated water during the 2001 tank experiment.*

Figure 17.—*The trees in this phytoremediation tank experiment grow better in the dirty water because one of the main contaminants is ammonia which acts as a fertilizer. This is part of why phytoremediation works.*

With this type of research, phytoremediation's promise has a better chance of being fulfilled, and the threat of unintended consequences can be reduced.

People-land connections, and understanding the interests of a heterogeneous population: Asset-based understanding of Calumet's communities

Revitalizing the economy and ecology of Calumet is not just in the hands of agency employees; it also depends on local residents. Therefore, it is important to understand the diverse local communities, their interests, their perceptions of the environment, and their connections to the land.

With support from NCRS, a team of ethnographers from Chicago's Field Museum of Natural History conducted applied anthropological research in several of Calumet's communities. Rather than looking at **needs**—the common starting point for a lot of community-based research—this research aimed at understanding the **assets** these communities have. Building on these assets can both strengthen the communities and shape and support the Calumet Initiative.

The Field Museum researchers identified numerous important assets that reflect community diversity and ties to the land of Calumet, including:

• **Hispanic community kinship networks.**— With regular meetings in homes or parks, kinship networks foster social networks and civic activism in the Hispanic community. This means that agency representatives who want to reach out to the Hispanic community need to find ways to work with these kinship networks just as they might work with church groups or Rotary Clubs to reach other segments of the population.

• **Gardening skills.**—In some neighborhoods, gardening is very popular: just about everyone has a garden at home and community gardens celebrate the local culture. This creates a point of common interest between local residents and land planning agencies. Gardening skills are also an asset that could be applied to local ecological restoration projects.

With an understanding of community assets and strengths, agencies are better able to partner with diverse community groups to meet both locally identified and regionally identified environmental goals.

SUMMARY AND FUTURE DIRECTIONS

In *The Nature of Tomorrow*, we asked three primary questions about riparian areas in the Midwest:

- How much do we have?
- Who's using these areas and what's happening to them? and
- How do we rehabilitate riparian landscapes?

We all use riparian areas, directly and indirectly.

Over the past several years, North Central Station scientists and our cooperators have begun to address these large questions. For the first time, we have an estimate of the amount of riparian land in our region, and a clearer sense of the difficulties involved in delineating the amount of riparian area and its land use. Current research will further our ability to delineate these delicate areas and to document their invaluable contributions to living the good life.

We all use riparian areas, directly and indirectly. Much of the food we eat and many of the products we use come from riparian areas. We seek riparian areas to live in; housing development in riparian areas has increased dramatically over the past decades. This development can create problems for the health of riparian and aquatic habitat. Our research has developed ways to predict development hotspots and to understand the important reasons that

people flock to the water's edge. With this understanding, we are better equipped to develop meaningful policies to protect our habitat and quality of life.

We also have developed tools and methods to improve riparian restoration and rehabilitation. From culvert placement to large planning efforts, our work helps practitioners improve ecosystem functions while providing benefits to their constituents. Phytoremediation promises to be a useful tool to clean up the messes in riparian and other settings.

We have learned a lot over these past several years, and we have much more to do. We need to replicate some of our recent studies to verify and strengthen the results and applications. We need to continue to refine delineation methods for riparian areas—without this we cannot be sure we are protecting the right places, or if we are over protecting these lands. We need to continue the search for ways to restore the health of riparian areas from the rustbelt to the remote reaches of the region.

The Riparian program was one of three *integrated* research programs at the North Central Research Station. There are several ways that research information can be integrated. The most common understanding of this—and the one at the core of our internal discussions as we developed the programs—is integration across disciplines. Historically, our research

> *We all need to know that the decisions made at the water's edge are sound and sustainable, because we depend on these intricate places— and they depend on us.*

was conducted in discipline-based units. The silviculture unit conducted silviculture studies, the wildlife unit wildlife studies, and so on. The intent of the integrated programs was to get us working across units to address major policy issues and conundrums. But there are other ways to achieve integration. Integration across scale is important; this aspect of integration is key to the National Science Foundation's Biocomplexity Initiative. Integration also can happen in the policymaker's head, where key information about constituent needs, biological necessities, and economic requirements come together and a decision is made. This is our bottom line: are we providing information to support sound decision making?

We have generated new riparian management and policy information that meets each of these integration criteria. We have integrated our work with seasonal wetlands across numerous disciplines and scales, from single cell organisms to stand-level understanding of these widespread, yet elusive, forest wetlands. By looking at both silviculture issues and geologic considerations, we were able to develop an easier way to determine where these wetlands are, thereby saving forest operators time and money as they follow riparian zone best management practices.

In our Calumet projects, we have integrated our work across disciplines and provided key information for policymakers as they strive to create both jobs and healthy habitat. Ethnographic studies of communities provide in-depth understanding of local issues and perspectives that foster more effective outreach and help policymakers incorporate the diverse perspectives of local residents in future plans for the region. Our work on creating ecologically friendly industrial sites

integrates landscape ecology, environmental psychology, and toxicology. This integration, for example, raised the possibility that concrete would, at times, be the most ecologically friendly landscape treatment if vegetation would threaten wildlife and workers with

Our work on creating ecologically friendly industrial sites integrates landscape ecology, environmental psychology, and toxicology.

transferred contamination. In the latest Calumet project, we have economists, conservation biologists, eco-toxicologists, planners, operation modelers, and others working together to integrate various disciplines and support decisions for on-the-ground rehabilitation of wetlands and other critical habitat.

Integration is a learned activity, and it can have a steep learning curve. Some of our early attempts to work in an integrated way were difficult. But we have learned, and we are not just getting better at it, we are very good at it. These pages reflect our success at developing new, useful, integrated information that helps you, the person in the decision making hot seat as you face tough decisions for our ecosystems and our world.

The work of the Riparian Integrated Program will continue in the new Northern Research Station. The issues will be addressed across all of the theme areas: clean air and water, urban natural resource stewardship, managing with disturbance, and sustaining forests.

If there are ways that we can be of further service, by all means, let us hear from you. We all need to know that the decisions made at the water's edge are sound and sustainable, because we depend on these intricate places—and they depend on us.

Appendix 1.—Riparian IP Project and Contact List

Bulleted items indicate a research agreement that is part of a larger NC study.

Project Title	Cooperating Institution	Unit	NC Contact/PI	Cooperator Contact/PI
Influence of large wood dams on stream organic matter processing and aquatic food webs in northern hardwood forest watersheds		NC-4101 Grand Rapids	Brian Palik 218-326-1711 bpalik@fs.fed.us	
• Large wood effects on stream organic matter processing and aquatic foodwebs in old-growth and second-growth forest watersheds	Bemidji State Univ.	NC-4101 Grand Rapids	Brian Palik 218-326-1711 bpalik@fs.fed.us	Richard Koch 218-755-2795 rkoch@bemidjistate.edu
• Geomorphic variation of large wood accumulation in old-growth and second-growth forest watersheds	Ohio State Univ.	NC-4101 Grand Rapids	Brian Palik 218-326-1711 bpalik@fs.fed.us	Charles Goebel 330-263-3789 goebel.11@osu.edu
Modeling the effects of riparian land use on ecological, economic, and social variables		NC-4101 Grand Rapids	Brian Palik 218-326-1711 bpalik@fs.fed.us	
Quantifying riparian areas in the Midwest Region		NC-4101 Grand Rapids	Brian Palik 218-326-1711 bpalik@fs.fed.us	
• Quantifying riparian areas in the Midwest Region	Bethel College	NC-4351 Grand Rapids	Brian Palik 218-326-1711 bpalik@fs.fed.us	Swee May Tang
Testing the efficacy of buffers for protecting seasonal ponds, amphibians, and songbirds in northern Minnesota forests		NC-4351 Grand Rapids	Brian Palik 218-326-1711 bpalik@fs.fed.us	
• Testing the efficacy of buffers for protecting aquatic invertebrates in seasonal ponds	North Dakota State Univ.	NC-4351 Grand Rapids	Brian Palik 218-326-1711 bpalik@fs.fed.us	Mark Hanson
• Testing the efficacy of buffers for protecting seasonal ponds and forest songbirds	Univ. of Minnesota	NC-4351 Grand Rapids	Brian Palik 218-326-1711 bpalik@fs.fed.us	Joann Hanowski 218-720-4311 jhanowsk@umn.edu
• Testing the efficacy of riparian buffers for protecting seasonal wetland hydrology	Univ. of Minnesota	NC-4101 Grand Rapids	Brian Palik 218-326-1711 bpalik@fs.fed.us	Jay Bell 612-625-6703
Effects of stream valley geomorphology on the composition and structure of riparian vegetation		NC-4101 Grand Rapids	Brian Palik 218-326-1711 bpalik@fs.fed.us	Kurt Pregitzer 906-487-2396 kspregit@mtu.edu
Riparian area delineation using a geomorphic approach		NC-4101 Grand Rapids	Brian Palik 218-326-1711 bpalik@fs.fed.us	
• Quantifying riparian areas in Minnesota using geomorphic indicators	Minnesota Dept. Nat. Resour.	NC-4351 Grand Rapids	Thomas Schmidt or Brian Palik	Tim Aunan

(Appendix 1 continued on next page)

Project Title	Cooperating Institution	Unit	NC Contact/PI	Cooperator Contact/PI
Using hydrogeomorphic processes to delineate riparian areas in the Little Carp (MI) and Popple River (WI) watersheds		NC-4101 Grand Rapids	Brian Palik 218-326-1711 bpalik@fs.fed.us	
Minnesota riparian management experiments				
• Multi-scale functional responses to stand manipulations in riparian forests	Univ. of Minnesota	NC-4101 Grand Rapids	Brian Palik 218-326-1711 bpalik@fs.fed.us	Eric Zenner 612-625-3733 ezenner@umn.edu
• Evaluating timber harvesting and forest management guidelines in riparian areas	Univ. of Minnesota	NC-4351 Grand Rapids	Brian Palik 218-326-1711 bpalik@fs.fed.us	Charlie Blinn 612-624-3788 cblinn@umn.edu
Defining stream valley segments in the National Forests of Wisconsin		NC-4351 Grand Rapids	Clay Edwards (retired) contact Randy Kolka 218-326-7115	
Distribution of in-lake coarse woody debris within old-growth and second-growth forest settings		NC-4351 Grand Rapids	Clay Edwards (retired) contact Randy Kolka 218-326-7115	
Effects of riparian development on habitat structure in north temperate lakes		NC-4351 Grand Rapids	Clay Edwards (retired) contact Randy Kolka 218-326-7115	
The influence of humans on colonization and extirpation processes in community assembly in small north temperate lakes		NC-4351 Grand Rapids	Clay Edwards (retired) contact Randy Kolka 218-326-7115	
• Establish a DNA map for muskellunges using microsatellite markers	Univ. of Wisconsin	NC-4351 Grand Rapids	Clay Edwards (retired) contact Randy Kolka 218-326-7115	Brian Sloss 715-346-3522
Afforestation of bottomland forests in Missouri		NC-4154 Columbia	Dan Dey 573-875-5341 x225 ddey@fs.fed.us	
The temporal ecology of coarse woody debris in aquatic and riparian ecosystems	Univ. of Missouri	NC-4154 Columbia	Dan Dey 573-875-5341, x225 ddey@fs.fed.us	Richard Guyette 573-882-7741 GuyetteR@missouri.edu
Modeling pre-European bottomland forest conditions of Missouri, along the Missouri River		NC-4154 Columbia	Dan Dey 573-875-5341 x225 ddey@fs.fed.us	Dr. Hong He 573-882-7717 heh@missouri.edu
Metropolitan trout streams: urban residents' perceptions and management of unique urban resources	Univ. of Minnesota	NC-4803 St. Paul	David Bengston 651-649-5162 dbengston@fs.fed.us	Kristin Nelson 612-624-1277 kcn@umn.edu
Intensive culture for restoration of agricultural floodplains		NC-4158 Rhinelander	Don Riemenschneider 715-362-1115 driemenschneider@fs.fed.us	

(Appendix 1 continued on next page)

Project Title	Cooperating Institution	Unit	NC Contact/PI	Cooperator Contact/PI
Riparian ecosystem assessment and management (REAM) project		NC-4154 Columbia	Frank Thompson 573-875-5341 x224 fthompson@fs.fed.us	
• Riparian ecosystem assessment monitoring project, heterofaunal monitoring	Missouri Dept. of Conserv.	NC-4154 Columbia	Frank Thompson 573-875-5341 x224 fthompson@fs.fed.us	Brian Root brian.root@mdc.mo.gov
Effects of riparian zone delineation and best management practices of landscape pattern and timber production	Univ. of Missouri	NC-4154, Columbia NC-4351, Grand Rapids	Steve Shifley and Brian Palik 218-326-1711 bpalik@fs.fed.us	Hong He 573-882-7717 heh@missouri.edu
Habitat benefits of riparian buffers in agricultural landscapes in Missouri		NC-4154 Columbia	Frank Thompson 573-875-5341 x224 fthompson@fs.fed.us	
Special places in the Calumet region		NC-4902 Evanston	Herb Schroeder 847-866-9311 x16 hschroeder@fs.fed.us	
Environmental factors influencing recreation choice in post-industrial landscapes	Purdue Univ.	NC-4902 Evanston	Herb Schroeder 847-866-9311 x16 hschroeder@fs.fed.us	David Klenosky 765-494-0865 DKlenosk@sla.purdue.edu
Assessment of physical and social implications of oxidized and reduced zones in soils of urban forests undergoing development	Texas A&M Univ.	NC-4902 Evanston	John Dwyer (retired) contact Herb Schroeder 847-866-9311 x16 hschroeder@fs.fed.us	Myron Floyd 352-392-4042 x1242 drfloyd@ufl.edu
Landscape level analysis linking urban sprawl and aquatic ecosystems	Univ. of Michigan	NC-4902 Evanston	John Dwyer (retired) contact Lynne Westphal 847-866-9311 x11 lwestphal@fs.fed.us	Daniel Brown 734-763-5803 danbrown@umich.edu
Phased phytoremediation strategy to protect Indian Ridge Marsh			Jud Isebrands (retired) contact Lynne Westphal 847-866-9311 x11 lwestphal@fs.fed.us	
• Phytoremediation potential for protecting Indian Ridge Marsh in the Calumet region of Chicago, IL	Univ. of Illinois	NC-4902 Evanston	Lynne Westphal 847-866-9311 x11 lwestphal@fs.fed.us	Marv Piwoni 217-244-8903 mpiwoni@wmrc.uiuc.edu
Carbon sequestration in riparian zones		NC-4152 Rhinelander	Jud Isebrands (retired) contact Neil Nelson 715-362-1153 nnelson@fs.fed.us	
Phytoremediation of streamside landfills using native trees		NC-4152 Rhinelander	Jud Isebrands (retired) contact Neil Nelson 715-362-1153 nnelson@fs.fed.us	

(Appendix 1 continued on next page)

Project Title	Cooperating Institution	Unit	NC Contact/PI	Cooperator Contact/PI
Phytoremediation of stream-side landfills		NC-4152 Rhinelander	Jud Isebrands (retired) contact Neil Nelson 715-362-1153 nnelson@fs.fed.us	
Testing willow clones for biomass production and streamside stabilization		NC-4152 Rhinelander	Jud Isebrands (retired) contact Neil Nelson 715-362-1153 nnelson@fs.fed.us	
Willow breeding program for biomass production and environmental benefits in riparian areas and uplands in the northeastern United States		NC-4152 Rhinelander	Jud Isebrands (retired) contact Neil Nelson 715-362-1153 nnelson@fs.fed.us	
Influence of belowground processes on carbon and nitrogen dynamics in a managed forested wetland	Michigan Tech. Univ.	NC-4159 Houghton	Kurt Pregitzer 906-487-2396 kkpregit@mtu.edu	Margaret Gab
Calumet Area Ecological Management Strategy		NC-4902 Evanston	Lynne Westphal 847-866-9311 x11 lwestphal@fs.fed.us	
Calumet area integrated database		NC-4902 Evanston	Lynne Westphal 847-866-9311 x11 lwestphal@fs.fed.us	
Calumet Research Summit		NC-4902 Evanston	Lynne Westphal 847-866-9311 x11 lwestphal@fs.fed.us	
User group perceptions, attitudes, and uses of open space in the Calumet region		NC-4902 Evanston	Lynne Westphal 847-866-9311 x11 lwestphal@fs.fed.us	
• Creating a digital record of the Calumet area riparian landscape	Univ. of Illinois	NC-4902 Evanston	Lynne Westphal 847-866-9311 x11 lwestphal@fs.fed.us	William Sullivan 217-244-5156 wcsulliv@staff.uiuc.edu
Calumet Region Angler Study	The Field Museum of Nat. History	NC-4902 Evanston	Lynne Westphal 847-866-9311 x11 lwestphal@fs.fed.us	Alaka Wali 312-665-7472 awali@fmnh.org
Aligning social and ecological drivers of urban landscape change in the Calumet urban riparian area	Univ. of Michigan	NC-4902 Evanston	Lynne Westphal 847-866-9311 x11 lwestphal@fs.fed.us	Joan Nassauer 734-763-9893 nassauer@umich.edu
Meaning, community and landscape change in Calumet	Univ. of Illinois	NC-4902 Evanston	Lynne Westphal 847-866-9311 x11 lwestphal@fs.fed.us	Daniel Cook 217-333-4410 dtcook@staff.uiuc.edu
Mapping social assets in the Lake Calumet region	The Field Museum of Nat. History	NC-4902 Evanston	Lynne Westphal 847-866-9311 x11 lwestphal@fs.fed.us	Alaka Wali 312-665-7472 awali@fmnh.org
Unearthing the benefits of Brownfield to Green Space Projects: a study of user and community perceptions and reactions	Univ. of Wisconsin	NC-4902 Evanston	Lynne Westphal 847-866-9311 x11 lwestphal@fs.fed.us	Christopher DeSousa 414-229-4874 desousa@uwm.edu

(Appendix 1 continued on next page)

Project Title	Cooperating Institution	Unit	NC Contact/PI	Cooperator Contact/PI
Calumet collaborative modeling project: Indian Ridge Marsh		NC-4902 Evanston	Lynne Westphal, 847-866-9311 x11 lwestphal@fs.fed.us Sarah McCaffrey	
• Developing a collaborative modeling approach to assess biological and economic effects of land use decisions	Univ. of Minnesota	NC-4902 Evanston	Lynne Westphal 847-866-9311 x11 lwestphal@fs.fed.us	Stephen Polasky 612-625-9213 polas004@umn.edu
Landscape change at Midewin Prairie	Univ. of Illinois	NC-4902 Evanston	Lynne Westphal 847-866-9311 x11 lwestphal@fs.fed.us	William Stewart 217-244-4532 wstewart@uiuc.edu
Making metropolitan areas more livable: recognizing and enhancing underappreciated natural resources	Univ. of Michigan	NC-4902 Evanston	Lynne Westphal 847-866-9311 x11 lwestphal@fs.fed.us	Rachel Kaplan 734-763-1061 rkaplan@umich.edu
Types and roles of fungal species near seasonal ponds in northern Minnesota		NC-4502 St. Paul	Mike Ostry 651-649-5113 mostry@fs.fed.us	
Analyzing linkages in Itasca County Lakes		NC-4803 St. Paul	Pam Jakes 651-649-5163 pjakes@fs.fed.us	
Developing an indexing framework to profile lake/riparian area development in northern Minnesota		NC-4803 St. Paul	Pam Jakes 651-649-5163 pjakes@fs.fed.us	
Developing an index framework to profile riparian area development in northern Minnesota	Univ. of Minnesota	NC-4803 St. Paul	Pam Jakes 651-649-5163 pjakes@fs.fed.us	Dorothy Anderson 612-624-2721 dha@umn.edu Clara Schlichting
Stakeholder of riparian ecosystem health in the Popple River Watershed, Wisconsin		NC-4803 St. Paul	Pam Jakes 651-649-5163 pjakes@fs.fed.us	
• Stakeholder perceptions of riparian ecosystem health	Univ. of Minnesota	NC-4803 St. Paul	Pam Jakes, John Dwyer, and Richard Buech	Dorothy Anderson 612-624-2721 dha@umn.edu
Predicting ecological and social impacts of riparian land use in a north central landscape	Univ. of Minnesota	NC-4803 St. Paul	Pam Jakes 651-649-5163 pjakes@fs.fed.us	Kristen Nelson 612-624-1277 kcn@umn.edu
Predicting ecological and social impacts of riparian land use in a riparian landscape	Univ. of Minnesota	NC-4803 St. Paul	Pam Jakes 651-649-5163 pjakes@fs.fed.us	Steven Polasky 612-624-9213 polas004@umn.edu Anthony Starfield 612-675-5721 starf001@umn.edu
Investigating factors limiting dispersal success by Waabizheski (American marten) in Wisconsin	Great Lakes Inidian Fish and Wildlife Comm.	NC-4153 Rhinelander	Patrick Zollner pzollner@fs.fed.us 715-362-1150	Jonathan Gilbert 715-682-6619 x121 jgilbert@glifwc.org

(Appendix 1 continued on next page)

Project Title	Cooperating Institution	Unit	NC Contact/PI	Cooperator Contact/PI
Negotiating nature in an urban park setting		NC-4902 Evanston	Paul Gobster pgobster@fs.fed.us 847-866-9311 x16 Sue Barro sbarro@fs.fed.us 651-649-5158	
Forest buffers at the urban fringe	Univ. of Illinois	NC-4902 Evanston	Paul Gobster 847-866-9311 x16 pgobster@fs.fed.us	William Sullivan 217-244-5156 wcsulliv@staff.uiuc.edu
Integrating social values in landscape change assessments	Iowa State Univ.	NC-4902 Evanston	Paul Gobster 847-866-9311 x16 pgobster@fs.fed.us	Mimi Wagner 515-294-8954 mimiw@iastate.edu
Post occupancy evaluation of urban park natural area restoration: Lincoln Park, Chicago, IL	Univ. of Illinois	NC-4902 Evanston	Paul Gobster 847-866-9311 x16 pgobster@fs.fed.us	Roberta Feldman 312-996-4717 rmf@uic.edu
Comparing perceptions of riparian function to assessed values and conditions: management in a changing landscape	Iowa State Univ.	NC-4902 Evanston	Paul Gobster 847-866-9311 x16 pgobster@fs.fed.us	Mimi Wagner 515-294-8954 mimiw@iastate.edu
Soil and landscape controls on the transport of septic tank effluent to surface waters and attenuation of nitrate	North Carolina State Univ.	NC-4351 Grand Rapids	Randy Kolka 218-326-7115 rkolka@fs.fed.us	Jim Thompson 919-513-0255 james_thompson@ncsu.edu
Hyporheic zone development and water quality improvement in a restored riparian area	Univ. of Kentucky	NC-4351 Grand Rapids	Randy Kolka 218-326-7115 rkolka@fs.fed.us	Christopher Barton 859-257-2099 barton@uky.edu
Retention and recruitment of coarse woody debris in high and low gradient streams in managed and old growth forests	Michigan Tech. Univ.	NC-4351 Grand Rapids	Randy Kolka 218-326-7115 rkolka@fs.fed.us	Marty Jurgensen 906-487-2206 mfjurgen@mtu.edu
Measuring coarse woody debris recruitment and assessing windthrow in riparian management zones in northern Minnesota	Univ. of Minnesota	NC-4351 Grand Rapids	Randy Kolka 218-326-7115 rkolka@fs.fed.us	Eileen Carey 612-624-7749 ecarey@umn.edu
Impacts of land use on channel morphology and stream habitat in northern Minnesota		NC-4351 Grand Rapids	E.S. Verry (retired) contact Randy Kolka 218-326-7115 rkolka@fs.fed.us	
• Stream morphological changes and their implications for floodplain management in the Minnesota River basin	Univ. of Minnesota	NC-4351 Grand Rapids	E.S.Verry (retired) contact Randy Kolka 218-326-7115 rkolka@fs.fed.us	Kenneth Brooks 612-624-2774 kbrooks@umn.edu
Stream-crossing designs for riparian restoration in Itasca County, MN		NC-4351 Grand Rapids	E.S. Verry (retired) contact Lynne Westphal 847-866-9311 x11 lwestphal@fs.fed.us	

(Appendix 1 continued on next page)

Project Title	Cooperating Institution	Unit	NC Contact/PI	Cooperator Contact/PI
Hydrological evaluation and stream rehabilitation recommendations for Indian Creek		NC-4351 Grand Rapids NC-4902 Evanston	E.S. Verry (retired) contact Lynne Westphal 847-866-9311 x11 lwestphal@fs.fed.us	
Identifying key linkages between water quality and land development patterns in riparian areas in the North Central Region	Univ. of Minnesota	NC-4803 St. Paul	Stephanie Snyder 651-649-5294 ssnyder@fs.fed.us	Larry Baker Mary Renwick 612-624-9282 baker127@umn.edu
Effects of riparian management practices on timber productivity, wildlife habitat, and landscape structure			Steve Shifley, 573-875-5341 x232 Hong He 573-882-7717	
Urban proximate second home use and amenity migration in Walworth County, WI		NC-4902 Evanston	Susan Stewart 847-866-9311 x13 sistewart@fs.fed.us	
Recreation and amenity migration in urban proximate areas	Loyola Univ.	NC-4902 Evanston	Susan Stewart 847-866-9311 x13 sistewart@fs.fed.us	Kenneth M. Johnson 773-508-3461 kjohnso@wpo.it.luc.edu
Second home owners and residents in the Hayward Lakes		NC-4902 Evanston	Susan Stewart 847-866-9311 x13 sistewart@fs.fed.us	
Demographic characteristics and population and housing unit projections in the Midwest Region	Univ. of Wisconsin	NC-4902 Evanston	Susan Stewart 847-866-9311 x13 sistewart@fs.fed.us	Roger Hammer 608-263-2898 rhammer@wisc.edu
Forest fragmentation due to housing changes in the northwoods spatial pattern of housing units through time	Univ. of Wisconsin	NC-4902 Evanston	Susan Stewart 847-866-9311 x13 sistewart@fs.fed.us	Volker Radeloff 608-263-4349 radeloff@wisc.edu
The role of riparian landowners in the management of Michigan's Manistee River	Michigan State Univ.	NC-4902 Evanston	Susan Stewart 847-866-9311 x13 sistewart@fs.fed.us	Charles Nelson 517-353-5190 x116 nelsonc@msu.edu
Land-use decisions on private lands: a study of land owners in the Upper Wabash River Basin	Purdue Univ.	NC-4902 Evanston	Susan Stewart 847-866-9311 x13 sistewart@fs.fed.us	Shorna Broussard 765-494-3603 srb@fnr.purdue.edu
Developing GIS simulation for integrating landscape ecological knowledge into landscape designs	Univ. of Michigan	NC-4902 Evanston	Susan Stewart 847-866-9311 x13 sistewart@fs.fed.us	Daniel G. Brown 734-763-5803 danbrown@umich.edu
Water quality as an indicator of landscape change	Iowa State Univ.	NC-4101 Grand Rapids	Thomas Crow (contact Randy Kolka 218-326-7115 rkolka@fs.fed.us)	Heidi Asbjornsen 515-294-7703 hasbjorn@iastate.edu

Appendix 2.—Sustaining Riparian Landscapes Publications and Related Products

Getting an Accurate Count: How Much Riparian Area Do We Have?

Palik, B.; Tang, Swee May; Chavez, Quinn. 2004. *Estimating riparian area extent and land-use in the Midwest United States.* Gen. Tech. Rep. NC-248. St. Paul, MN: U.S. Department of Agriculture, Forest Service, North Central Research Station. 25 p.

Palik, B.; Buech, R.; Egeland, L. 2003. *Using an ecological land hierarchy to predict the abundance of seasonal wet-lands in northern Minnesota forests.* Ecological Applications. 13: 1153-1163.

Who's Using and What's Happening to Riparian Areas?

Batzer, D.P.; Palik, B.; Buech, R. 2004. *Relationships between environmental characteristics and macroinvertebrate communities in seasonal woodland ponds of Minnesota.* Journal of the North American Benthological Society. 23: 50-68.

Brawn, J.D.; Robinson, S.K.; Thompson, F.R., III. 2001. *The role of disturbance in the ecology and conservation of birds.* Annual Review of Ecology and Systematics. 32: 251-276.

Brown, D.G.; Duh, J.D. 2004. *Using spatial simulation to translate between land use and land cover.* International Journal of Geographical Information Science. 18(1): 35-60.

Cifaldi, R.; Allan, J.D.; Duh, J.D.; Brown, D.G. 2004. *Spatial patterns in land cover of exurbanizing watersheds in southeastern Michigan.* Landscape and Urban Planning. 66(2): 107-123.

Fish, T.E. 2001. *Landowner perceptions of ecosystem health in Upper Great Lakes states riparian landscapes.* St. Paul, MN: University of Minnesota. 178 p. Unpublished Ph.D. dissertation.

Fish, T.E.; Anderson, D.H.; Jakes, P.J. 2001. *Identifying disparities between public perceptions and technical knowledge in Great Lakes riparian ecosystems.* In: Proceedings of the Coastal Zone '01; Cleveland, OH. Charleston, SC: U.S. Department of Commerce, National Oceanic and Atmospheric Administration, Coastal Services Center.

Fish. T.E.; Anderson, D.H.; Jakes, P.J. 2000. *Landowner perceptions of riparian ecosystem health in the upper Great Lakes states.* In: Taylor, J.G.; Shelby, L.B., eds. The 11th International conference of the Society for Human Ecology: book of abstracts. Bar Harbor, ME: The Society for Human Ecology: 46. Abstract.

Fishwick, L.; Vining, J. 1992. *Toward a phenomenology of recreation place.* Journal of Environmental Psychology. 12: 57-63.

Gobster, P.H.; Barro, S.C. 2000. *Negotiating nature: making restoration happen in an urban park context.* In: Gobster, P.H.; Hull, R.B., eds. Restoring nature: perspectives from the social sciences and humanities. Washington DC: Island Press: 185-207.

Gobster, P.H.; Westphal, L.M. 2004. *The human dimensions of urban greenways: planning for recreation and related experiences.* Landscape and Urban Planning. 68: 147-165.

Goebel, P.C.; Palik, B.; Pregitzer, K. 2003. *Geomorphic influences on large wood dam loadings, particulate organic matter and dissolved organic matter in an old-growth northern hardwood watershed.* Journal of Freshwater Ecology. 18: 479-490.

Goebel, P.C.; Palik, B.; Pregitzer, K. 2004. *Plant diversity contributions of riparian areas in watersheds of the northern Lake States.* Ecological Applications. 13: 1595-1609.

Gustafson, E.J.; Murphy, N.L.; Crow, T.R. 2001. *Using a GIS model to assess terrestrial salamander response to alternative forest management plans.* Journal of Environmental Management. 63: 281-292.

Hammitt, W.E. 2002. *Urban forests and parks as privacy refuges.* Journal of Arboriculture. 28(1): 19-26.

Jakes, Pamela J.; Schlichting, Ciara; Anderson, Dorothy H. 2003. *A framework for profiling a lake's riparian area development potential.* Journal of Environmental Management. 69: 391-400.

Jennings, M.J.; Emmons, E.E.; Hatzenbeler, G.R.; Edwards, C.; Bozek, M.A. 2003.
Is littoral habitat affected by residential development and land use in watersheds of Wisconsin lakes? Lake and Reservoir Management. 19(3): 272-279.

Nassauer, J.I.; Kosek, S.E.; Corry, R.C. 2001.
Meeting public expectations with ecological innovation in riparian landscapes. Journal of the American Water Resources Association. 37(6): 1-5.

Palik, B.; Cease, K.; Egeland, L.; Blinn, C. 2003.
Aspen regeneration in riparian management zones in northern Minnesota: effects of residual overstory and harvest method. Northern Journal of Applied Forestry. 20: 79-84.

Peak, R.G. 2002.
Factors affecting avian species richness, density, and nest success in riparian corridors. Columbia, MO: University of Missouri-Columbia. 72 p. Unpublished M.S. thesis.

Peak, R.G.; Thompson, F.R.; Shaffer, T.L. 2004.
Factors affecting songbird nest survival in riparian forests in a Midwestern agricultural landscape. The Auk. 121(3): 726-737.

Perry, J.; Blinn, C.; Newman, R.; *et al.* 2001.
Evaluating riparian area dynamics, management alternatives and impacts of harvest practices. Final Report to the Minnesota Forest Resources Council and the National Council on Air and Stream Improvement.

Rust, A.J.; Diana, J.S.; Margenau, T.L.; Edwards, C.J. 2002.
Lake characteristics influencing spawning success of muskellunge in northern Wisconsin lakes. North American Journal of Fisheries Management. 22: 834-841.

Schlichting, C. 2001.
A framework to profile lake riparian development: an application to Itasca County, Minnesota. St. Paul, MN: University of Minnesota. Unpublished M.S. thesis.

Schroeder, H.W. 2002.
Experiencing nature in special places: surveys from the North-Central Region. Journal of Forestry. 100(5): 8-14.

Stewart, W.P.; Liebert, D.; Larkin, K.W. 2004.
Community identities as visions for landscape change. Landscape and Urban Planning. 69: 315-334.

Sullivan, William C.; Anderson, Olin M.; Kivekkm Sara Taylor. 2004.
Agricultural buffers at the rural-urban fringe: an examination of approval by farmers, residents, and academics in the Midwestern United States. Landscape and Urban Planning. 69: 299-313.

Thompson, F.R., III; DeGraaf, R.M. 2001.
Conservation approaches for woody, early successional communities in the eastern United States. Wildlife Society Bulletin. 29: 483-494.

How Do We Rehabilitate Riparian Areas

City of Chicago. Department of Environment. 2002.
Calumet area ecological management strategy. Chicago, IL: City of Chicago, Department of Environment. 170 p.

Dey, D.C.; Guyette, R.; Stambaugh, M. 2003.
Ancient wood uncovered. Missouri Conservationist. 64(1): 4-7.

Dey, D.; Kabrick, J.; Grabner, J.; Gold, M. 2002.
Reforesting oaks in the Missouri River floodplain. In: Proceedings, 29th Annual hardwood symposium: hardwood silviculture and sustainability: 2001 and beyond; 2001 May 17-19; French Lick, IN. Memphis, TN: National Hardwood Lumber Association: 8-20.

Dey, D.C.; Kabrick, J.M.; Gold, M.A. 2003.
Establishing oaks in Big River floodplains. Missouri Society of American Foresters. Missouri Forestry Newsletter. 19(1): 3-5.

Dey, D.C.; Kabrick, J.M.; Gold, M.A. 2003.
Tree establishment in floodplain agroforestry practices. In: Proceedings, 8th North American agroforestry conference; 2003 June 22-25; Corvallis, OR: Oregon State University: 102-115.

Dey, D.; Burhans, D.; Kabrick, J.; Root, B.; Grabner, J.; Gold, M. 2000.
The Missouri River floodplain: history of oak forests and current restoration efforts. The Glade. 3(2): 2-4.

Dugger, S.; Dey, D.C.; Millspaugh, J.J. 2004.
Vegetation cover affects mammal herbivory on planted oaks and success of reforesting Missouri river Bottomland Fields. In: Connor, K.F., ed. Proceedings, 12th Biennial southern silvicultural conference; 2003 February 24-28; Biloxi, MS. Gen. Tech. Rep. SRS-71. Asheville, NC: U.S. Department of Agriculture, Forest Service, Southern Research Station: 3-6.

Edwards, Clay; *et al.* 1998.
Aquatic zoogeography of North America (Nearctic Zone). 2d approximation. Available on the Great Lakes Assessment Web site: http://www.ncrs.fs.fed.us/gla/

Grossman, B.C.; Gold, M.A.; Dey, D.C. 2001.
Restoration of hard mast species for wildlife in Missouri floodplains: precocious flowering in Quercus. In: Proceedings, 7th North American agroforestry conference; 2001 August 12-15; Regina, Saskatchewan: 233-242.

Grossman, B.C.; Gold, M.A.; Dey, D.C. 2003.
Effect of acorn mass and size, and early shoot growth on one-year old container-grown RPM™ oak seedlings. In: Van Sambeek, J.W.; et al., eds. Proceedings, 13th Central Hardwood forest conference; 2002 April 1-3; Urbana-Champaign, IL. Gen. Tech. Rep. NC-234. St. Paul, MN: U.S. Department of Agriculture, Forest Service, North Central Research Station: 405-414.

Grossman, B.C.; Gold, M.A.; Dey, D.C. 2003.
Restoration of hard mast species for wildlife in Missouri using precocious flowering oak in the Missouri River Floodplain. USA Agroforestry Systems. 59: 3-10.

Guyette, R.; Dey, D.C. 2001.
Ancient wood uncovered. Missouri Society of American Foresters, Missouri Forestry Newsletter. 17(2): 3-4.

Guyette, R.P.; Stambaugh, M.C.; Dey, D.C. 2003.
Fire history in the riparian corridor of the Ozark National Scenic Riverways: a report for the National Park Service. Van Buren, MO: Ozark National Scenic Riverways. 24 p. with illus.

Guyette, R.P.; Cole, W.G.; Dey, D.C.; Muzika, R.M. 2002.
Perspectives on the age and distribution of large wood in riparian carbon pools. Canadian Journal of Fisheries and Aquatic Sciences. 59: 578-585.

Kabrick, J.; Dey, D. 2001.
Silvics of Missouri bottomland tree species. Notes for For. Managers Rep. #5. Jefferson City, MO: Missouri Department of Conservation. 8 p.

Nelson, E.A.; Kolka, R.K.; Trettin, C.C.; Wisniewski, J., eds. 2000.
Restoration of the severely impacted riparian wetland system. Ecological Engineering. 15 (Suppl. 1): 189 p.

Shaw, G.W.; Dey, D.C.; Kabrick, J.; Grabner, J.; Muzika, R.M. 2003.
Comparison of site preparation methods and stock types for artificial regeneration of oaks in bottomlands. In: Van Sambeek, J.W.; et al., eds. Proceedings, 13th Central Hardwood forest conference; 2002 April 1-3; Urbana-Champaign, IL. Gen. Tech. Rep. NC-234. St. Paul, MN: U.S. Department of Agriculture, Forest Service, North Central Research Station: 186-198.

Smith, W.P.; Zollner, P.A. 2001.
Seasonal habitat distribution of mammals in an old-growth bottomland hardwood forest. In: Hamel, P.B.; Foti, T., eds. Bottomland hardwoods of the Mississippi Alluvial Valley: characteristics and management of natural function. Gen. Tech. Rep. SRS-42. Asheville, NC: U.S. Department of Agriculture, Forest Service, Southern Research Station: 83-99.

Verry, E.S. 2001.
Hydrologic evaluation and stream restoration for Indian Creek (based on survey field work). Grand Rapids, MN: U.S. Department of Agriculture, Forest Service, North Central Research Station. 62 p.

Verry, Elon S.; *et al.* 2003.
Identifying Bankfull Stage in forested streams in the Eastern United States. Fort Collins, CO: U.S. Department of Agriculture, Forest Service. Stream Systems Technology Center. 46 minute video.

Wali, A.; Darlow, G.; Fialkowski, C.; Tudor, M.; del Campo, H.; Stotz, D. 2003.
New methodologies for interdisciplinary research and action in an urban ecosystem in Chicago. Conservation Ecology. 7(3): 11 p.

Westphal, L.M.; Isebrands, J.G. 2001.
Phytoremediation of Chicago's brownfields: consideration of ecological approaches and social issues. In: Brownfield 2001; 2001 September 24-26; Chicago, IL. [Available only online: http://www.brownfields2002.org/proceedings#2001/naviation.pdf.]

MISSION STATEMENT

We believe the good life has its roots in clean air, sparkling water, rich soil, healthy economies and a diverse living landscape. Maintaining the good life for generations to come begins with everyday choices about natural resources. The North Central Research Station provides the knowledge and the tools to help people make informed choices. That's how the science we do enhances the quality of people's lives.